MAYAN CIVII

A History from Beginning to End

Copyright © 2016 by Henry Freeman

All rights reserved.

The cover photo is a derivative of

"Chichen Itza 3" (https://en.wikipedia.org/wiki/File:Chichen_Itza_3.jpg) by Daniel Schwen, used under CC BY-SA 4.0 (https://creativecommons.org/licenses/by-sa/4.0/deed.en),

"Dintel 26 de Yachilán 3" (https://commons.wikimedia.org/wiki/File:Dintel_26_de_Yachil%C3%A1n_3.jpg) by ProtoplasmaKid, used under CC BY-SA 4.0 (**https://creativecommons.org/licenses/by-sa/4.0/deed.en**).

"Maya-Maske" (https://en.wikipedia.org/wiki/File:Maya-Maske.jpg) by Wolfgang Sauber, used under CC BY-SA 3.0 (https://creativecommons.org/licenses/by-sa/3.0/deed.en).

Table of Contents

Who Made Contact? Early Explorers and Their Impact
How the Maya Wanted to Be Represented—History Written by the Victors
Different Periods of Maya History
Larger Than Life
New Findings

Introduction

The Mayan civilization perceived a highly-structured cosmos, reflected in most aspects of their practices and societies. In today's world, humans live in so many different environments that have played a role in developing their cultures, sustenance and philosophies. We can stand in the middle of our street, our yard, a field, on top of a mountain, or inside a museum, close our eyes and try to imagine what that particular spot looked like throughout time. Who roamed these lands before us? Such thoughts can send us on a voyage of discovery. Depending on how close our ties are to where we live, we may shed a tear from nostalgia and from an appreciation of our ever-changing landscapes and lives. We may ask those who are more familiar with the history of that place and seek answers through research.

Our detective work may include looking at the nature of things. What was here before this very tree? Did the sky look the same through ancient Maya eyes as it might if we stood next to them in their sacred rainforests? Do the millions of Maya of various ethnic groups—the inheritors of the Maya traditions and their past—now stand in awe in the same places where their ancestors stood, despite the newest political borders in their beloved Mesoamerican homelands? If they practiced the same way of life in ancient times, even if the practices today of our own times are quite different, can we find any long lost awareness and understanding about how they grappled with common human fears, problems and questions?

As humans, we love to determine what has come before. Our natural curiosity drives us to grapple with the shape of the things we see in the environment, the structures, and the land, and to visualize the changes that often span generations. We wonder who else has been here. What animals hunted and what birds permeated the air with their cries as ancient humans went about their lives? How did they live? We want history to come alive just as much as we want to be able to establish our sense of the world.

The Maya people shared that curiosity. They imagined their world in such a way that helped them develop a way of thinking. It ensured good harvests, protection for the commoners, great victories for their kings, and soothed their gods. The ceiba tree grew deep in the Central American rainforest. It was sacred. The Maya considered it the first tree or the world tree. As the center of the Earth, even to this day, the ceiba tree is often left undisturbed out of respect. The tree held significant power over the Maya. It was referred to in the eighteenth century Chilam Balam, a chronicle that was written in the Yucatan that may have been originally transcribed from hieroglyphic texts into a Mayan language. The sacred tree was thought to bridge the gap between the earthly realm and the spirit realm. The Maya routinely represented the thorny trunks of the ceiba tree in their ceramic pots, used as burial urns or incense holders.

Continuing on these traditions recently, colorful spiked ceramic funeral urns known as MT Objects were designed by Mexico City-based designers in the spring of 2016, inspired by the Mayan beliefs surrounding the Ceiba tree. Advancing the Maya's practice of borrowing from nature isn't the only thing that has been noticed about the significance they placed on the world they inhabited. The ceiba tree is a national symbol of Guatemala and was declared the national tree of the country in 1955, in part because of its importance to the Maya. They are protected by Guatemalan law. One of the most famous ceiba trees is found in Palin, Escuintla, and it is more than 400 years old.

Many towns are named after the tree throughout Central America, the Caribbean, and Mexico.

The Maya added sacred significance to the natural wonders of the environment. In the Popol Vuh, one of the world's greatest creation accounts and the Maya early version of the human story that is considered deeply satisfying on an emotional level, the Maya held that everything had a sacred element to it. All material objects were constructed from elements of creation. "Pop" is the word for this interdependent fabric of life. According to Andres Xiloj, a trained ritual specialist, one of the introductory passages described that the gods measured out the surface of the earth as though it were a cornfield being laid out for cultivation. Karen Bassie-Sweet further described how the world looked to the Maya in "Maya Sacred Geography and the Creator Deities." The deities created and destroyed the quadrilateral world several times. They would eventually destroy and recreate it again. Each year, the Maya validated their world model based on the corn cycle, since every year they destroyed wild spaces with cutting and burning and transformed them into corn fields. This interlocking view translated into the structures of communities that they built and their systems of governance and trade.

For 2,000 years, from 1100 BCE to 1500 CE, the Maya ruled their civilization in modern-day El Salvador, western Honduras, Guatemala, Belize and parts of southern Mexico. They established a bigger than life civilization in the rainforests, along the coasts, in the lowlands and highlands. Those who inherited their history continue to live in the same region, despite being conquered, absorbed over time and deprived of the historical accounts of their ancestors which were destroyed during the years of the Spanish Conquest. As Archaeology magazine editor Zach Zorich once noted, "Among the Maya, the victors literally did write the history. Rulers were proud to commemorate their successful military campaigns, while the losers typically did not record their defeats."

Yet, even after reviewing all the works that focus on the Maya, what we know about the people and their culture is based on the emphasis on the mystery of their decline. While it is certainly a critical mystery that is up for debate, and one we will also consider given newer discoveries, this amplification of one portion of their timeline sometimes neglects what they have inspired and the awe-provoking, and sometimes terrifying, lives they led. In fact, some of their practices we would not connect with, while others seem to make sense rationally.

There is much to learn about the internal warfare between city-states within the Mayan civilization that will shed light on the complex history of the Maya. While the Maya were thought to be peacefully separated into 40 independent city-states for years, continual research, archaeological finds and revisited theories in the last half-century have dismantled this hypothesis. Evidence of a much more brutal civilization has updated our impression of the Maya. This will be discussed in the following pages.

Over the course of generations, the ancient Maya did more than build massive pyramids (without the help of beasts of burden), construct complicated calendars and study the stars. In the early period, their shamans made informal decisions for their societies until the role of leadership transformed into the institutionalized rule of kings. They developed trade zones, a barter system of exchange, and a concept of beauty that many around the world find unique. While their spiritual and dynastic history is fascinating and well explored, their scientific discoveries are considered some of humankind's greatest achievements. They had the misfortune of meeting Christopher Columbus when he traveled to Honduras.

Unintentionally, he became the gateway for introducing Europe to chocolate, despite how differently the Maya and Aztecs had prepared it themselves for their own ritualist and medicinal uses. They attracted the attention of famous American writer Edgar Allan Poe in 1841 and led American aviator Charles "Lucky Lindy" Lindbergh to pilot two reconnaissance flights in 1929.

This book will share some interesting facts about the Maya and their encounter with Columbus, as well as the attention these well-known Americans brought to the Maya, which fascinated the world. They were so successful in building their civilization that they may very well have become victims of their success.

As you imagine yourself in their shoes in the Yucatan, Chichen Itza, western Honduras or in front of Christopher Columbus, consider what it must have felt like to them to find out that there were civilizations beyond the scope of their trade routes. These are a people that would find their way of life changed forever, leading those who inherited their legacy to piece together what the Spanish destroyed in the 1500s. Also, consider this: when the Spanish arrived in the 1580s, along the Caribbean coast, a Franciscan priest and his secretary Antonio de Ciudad Real asked some Indians, "What's the name of this place? How did it get its name?" In response, the Indians said *uic athan,* which means, "what do you say" or "what do you speak?" In other words, the Maya didn't understand them. Ciudad Real wrote, "The Spaniard ordered it set down to be called Yucatan."

Getting lost in translation set the tone for the meeting of the minds between the West and the New World, and despite how much people hope that a first impression might be a good one, it appears that given their extremely conflicting interests, the Maya may have found themselves stumped by the Europeans—and not just in this episode.

Stephen Greenblatt, in his 1991 book "Marvelous Possessions: The Wonder of the New World," wrote, "The Maya expression of incomprehension becomes the colonial name of the land that is wrested from them."

Although the ancient Maya might have had an extremely rude awakening when they began to gather what the Spaniards came for, they did put up a fight, despite the advantages their colonizing foes had in weaponry. It's highly recommended to continue your exploration of the Maya world by learning more about the Spanish Conquest and the various resources that explore that time period in history. The world must have looked much smaller as their sacred land became in the minds of the Spaniards a conquered one, without the cultural significance that the Maya could no longer preserve. Despite history, the attempts to rebuild the world of the Maya as they saw it are numerous and fascinating when connected.

Chapter One
Who Made Contact? Early Explorers and Their Impact

As we will further explore later in this book, the Maya had developed long-distance trade before and during what is considered the decline of their civilization, when their populations shifted. Before we consider inner-cultural and inter-cultural trade among those who made pre-Columbian Mesoamerica their homes, it's worth considering what initial contact with Europeans was like for the Mayan civilization. Christopher Columbus arrived on July 30, 1502, at Guanaja, which is one of the Bay Islands off the northern coast of modern-day Honduras. He knew nothing about the lives, hearts, accomplishments and ways of the Maya. Before his historic landing in Honduras, he stopped a Chontal Maya trading canoe in the Bay of Honduras. The Chontal Maya lived on the coast of the Yucatan Peninsula and bartered jaguar skins, cacao beans, feathers, and tortoiseshells in exchange for salt, copper, lumber and corn. This first Spanish encounter with Maya was not a friendly one.

Where was Columbus headed and what had he left behind in Spain to take this journey? Columbus had been convinced, after reading Marco Polo's account of voyaging westward through the South China Sea, that Cuba was part of China. He hoped he would manage to find a strait connecting the Caribbean to the Indian Ocean. According to Martin Dugard in "The Last Voyage of Columbus: Being the Epic Tale of the Great Captain's Fourth Expedition, Including Accounts of Swordfight, Mutiny, Shipwreck, Gold, War, Hurricane, and Discovery," "Columbus's certainty that he was in Asia was grounded in the maps of Ptolemy, the writings of Marco Polo, his own experiences at sea, the Bible, and a slew of other sources." This was his fourth voyage in search of China.

Although he never found China, Columbus set the stage for the Spanish conquest of many Mesoamerican societies. His fourth voyage was approved by Spain's Queen Isabella as part of the Spanish crown's pursuit of establishing the country as the first global power to dominate Europe and much of the world. He received her approval, despite his home arrest in 1500, for his previous mismanagement of the Spanish colony Hispaniola, which had left his reputation in tatters.

In 1502, Columbus had no idea that by the Classic period, the Maya had, as a collective whole, developed an extensive trade network that stretched from the Yucatan to Honduras. Between 900 and 300 BCE, the Maya are said to have experienced the period of greatest achievement in their southern lowlands region. Pre-Columbian Maya lived in an area that extended from the Mexican states of Chiapas and Tabasco north to the tip of the Yucatan Peninsula and east through Guatemala into Honduras and El Salvador. Their geographical area was basically the size of New Mexico. Columbus and those who accompanied him had no idea that the Maya had experienced a decline that began in the tenth and eleventh centuries that would be the subject of extensive future debate.

Columbus had been on his final voyage to the New World. At the same time, the Maya were living among the ruins of their once great civilization during what historians, anthropologists and archaeologists consider the Post-Classic period. The Late Postclassic period, from 1200 to 1524, has been characterized as being notable for the relative absence of the immense cities that had defined the Maya Classic period that represent the majority of tourist sites today. The Maya were now politically less centralized, and warfare among many competing petty states was a constant occurrence. Mayapan and Tulum were key cities in the Northern region during this period. By the time of his arrival, the royal city of Copan, northwest Honduras' most famous Maya site, had already been reclaimed by the jungle.

The Northern area was densely populated and commercially active. Maritime trade along coastal towns and Belizean rivers allowed the Maya to circumnavigate the entire Yucatan Peninsula, from the Gulf of Mexico to Belize and Honduras on the Caribbean. The Maya had established some 150 coastal sites by the time of the Spanish conquest, following Columbus' initial contact. His observations of the Yucatan Maya led the Spaniards to conquer the Maya areas after several Spanish exploration missions. The Maya did not know much about the Caribbean islands beyond their horizon. Those who have investigated the reasons they did not venture further to find Europe themselves suggest that it had much to do with the trade winds, which winds blew steadily south and west, defeating any attempt to sail against them. As Laurence Bergreen observed in "Columbus: The Four Voyages, 1492-1504," Columbus benefited greatly from the prevailing winds.

According to Columbus' journals, he had an inkling that the people he encountered were part of a powerful and ancient civilization, but since they were not Chinese, they did not interest him. He noted their great seamanship and their long canoe-like crafts. He detained one person, a man named Yumbé, as his guide. He continued to Cabo Gracias a Dios and all the way to present-day Panama. There he dropped his unlucky captive and returned to Spain. There, they looted the boat and tore off the fine clothing of the men and pawed at the women. Columbus' son Fernando, who became his biographer, described the degradation of the Maya and boasted of how they took the costliest and handsomest things in that cargo including weapons, copper and grains, including a "wine made of maize that tasted like English beer."

Ironically, the cacao beans that the Maya carried did not interest the Spaniards on this trip, despite how important they seemed to the "Indians" who "squatted down to pick them up as if they had lost something of great value." Columbus did, however, bring a handful of the beans back to Spain. Considered by the Maya as the food of the gods, it wouldn't be until years later after Cortez conquered Montezuma's Aztec empire that chocolate and the process for making it—a process which differed from the Maya tradition of drinking it—became a fad. The Maya enjoyed chocolate, usually unsweetened, as a frothy drink that was considered a very valuable commodity in trade. It would grow to become a sweeter version enjoyed by the Spanish in 1528, despite having been introduced to the cacao bean that day. It wouldn't be shared with the rest of the Europeans for 100 years.

On August 14, 1502, Columbus landed in Trujillo on the coast of Honduras. The Lenca were the dominant cultural group in the region—several tribes inhabited the country, including the Pech and Sumu tribes and the Tolupan, Pipils and Chorotega. They maintained commercial relations among themselves and with other indigenous populations from Mexico to Panama.

After Columbus's first contact with the Maya, other Spanish explorers visited the region to explore Maya sites. In 1511, a Spanish sailing ship ran aground off of Jamaica and sank. More than 20 crew members drifted on a lifeboat for thirteen days until they made it to the Yucatan coast. According to an account by Diego de Landa, several of these men were sacrificed by the Maya people they encountered. He had been sent to bring the Catholic religion to the native people. Geronimo de Aguilar, a priest, and Gonzalo Guerrero, a sailor, were the only ones who survived. In later years, de Landa burned more than 5,000 Maya images and dozens of Maya books that he believed to be works of the devil. The texts that did survive will be discussed in the next chapter.

In 1517, Francisco Hernandez de Cordoba led a Spanish expedition that was meant to capture slaves to work in the gold and silver mines in Cuba. On the island Isla de las Mujeres off the northeastern Yucatan, named so after the Maya goddess statues he found there, Cordoba was forced to retreat to Cuba after a final battle with Maya warriors led by Mochcouoh. Under his leadership, the warriors killed twenty Spaniards and captured two more. Cordoba, suffering from numerous wounds, had to flee despite his earlier battle gains. His accounts of wealth, clothed natives and relative sophistication in practices and construction of the Maya drew the attention of other Spaniards.

In 1519, the infamous Spanish conquistador Hernan Cortes left Cuba with eleven ships and 500 men and headed to the "island of swallows"—Cozumel, on the eastern coast of Yucatan. They attacked one town and announced they had arrived to pick up other bearded men in an attempt to recover the two survivors from 1511. At this point, Geronimo de Aguilar had been living among the Maya of Yucatan for eight years. The Spanish proceeded into battles with Maya forces, capturing Potonchan and Centla and leading eventually to the Maya submitting to Spanish rule. That same year, Cortes would meet the Aztec king Montezuma, invade Mexico, and within two years would conquer the Aztec empire.

To get some insight into what the Maya people might have been thinking after noticing Spanish exploration in their territories, it's not surprising that the Maya and other indigenous groups weren't just standing there scratching their heads. Lynn Foster in "Handbook to Life in the Ancient Maya World" noted that when the Spaniards first started exploring Mesoamerica in the early 16th century, the Aztec emperor Moctezuma (known as Montezuma more popularly) suggested to the Highland Maya that they should consolidate their forces against the Europeans. Unfortunately, despite the attempt to ally with one another, they were defeated, and the capital of Tenochtitlan was destroyed by the Spaniards. It's also worth mentioning that prior to building an alliance, the Aztecs were known to encroach on the Maya region, which led to significant battles. Despite their ambitions to build their empire, the Aztecs were the engine that drove much of Maya trade during the 15th century.

There are even extant Maya codices that have been preserved that suggest prophetic stories led to Montezuma surrendering to Cortes, with the Aztec ruler's own diviners predicting the European invasions. Additionally, the Mayan sacred text, the Book of Chilam Balam, foretold the Spanish invasion, the conquest of the Maya and future suffering of the oppressed people. According to many experts, the prophet Chilam Balam anticipated the arrival of Spaniards and Christianity in order to prepare them for imminent change. According to some interpretations of the Florentine Codex, compiled by the Franciscan friar Bernardino de Sahagun between 1547 and 1569, there were signs and bad omens that appeared to the Aztecs before the Spanish came to attack the area. There are many available interpretations of the conquest being anticipated and preordained.

In exploring the impact the early explorers and the conquests had on the Maya, there are some excellent resources available that provide not only the victor accounts, but also the non-colonial accounts from Mayan sources. Many of these offer a fascinating look at the historical events that led to colonial expansion and consolidation. For example, Matthew Restall's "Maya Conquistador" explores these perspectives in comparison to Spanish accounts; Inga Clendinnen, in "Ambivalent Conquests: Maya and Spaniard in Yucatan, 1517-1570", sheds light on the experience of the Maya following the arrival of the Spaniards in the Americas, the resistance movement and breaks from silencing their interpretations so that they do not remain unexplored.

Chapter Two

How the Maya Wanted to Be Represented—History Written by the Victors

The impression lingers that the Mayan civilization was a homogenous group that was subsumed by the Spanish conquerors. While that might be a place to start, we only scratch the surface with this representation of Mayan roots. While the earliest Maya share a single language, by the Preclassic Period, from 2000 to 250 BCE, they developed a wide variety of languages among various Maya peoples. Twenty-eight languages are known, based on various inhabited locations. It's hard not to appreciate that another impression of the Maya people is based on their relationship to nature, where everything is instilled with a sacredness, a vital spirituality that has lent to their culture a respect for nature and the world that Western civilizations can learn from.

However true that may be, what's been left out of the narrative is the animal sacrifices and the environmental damage caused by their civilization that lingers into today. In other words, it's not easy to use broad brush strokes to capture the life and times of an ancient civilization with a complex society, especially one that weaved a complex web of culture that bore many fruits from their labor for us to explore.

Many archaeologists, historians, anthropologists, and ethnohistorians have scoured scores of documents that remain from the era of the Spanish Conquest, including Franciscan accounts that pre-date the infamous account written by New York lawyer John Lloyd Stephens and architect Frederick Catherwood. Stephens and Catherwood are credited for largely bringing the attention of the outside of the world to the Mayan civilization circa 1850. The famous American writer Edgar Allen Poe reviewed three of Stephens' books and called the instant bestseller "Incidents of Travel in Yucatan" "perhaps the most interesting book of travel ever published."

The Popol Vuh, a nearly 500-year-old Mayan text written in Quiche, still remains an excellent source of knowledge about the ancient Maya, despite the forced conformity that the Maya experienced during the Spanish conquest to accept Christianity and reject their nativism, religion, and spiritual practices. It is still considered an important part of the belief system of many Maya and was used extensively for divining and decision making.

In early 2016, Pope Francis during his visit to San Cristobal Da Las Casas, Mexico, cited the Popol Vuh and said a few words in one of the native indigenous Maya languages to a crowd during a ceremony that included women chanting hymns in the Chol, Tzotzil, and Tzeltal Mayan languages. According to press reports, the Pope said, "On many occasions, in a systematic and organized way, your people have been misunderstood and excluded from society. Some have considered your values, culture, and traditions to be inferior. Others, intoxicated by power, money and market trends, have stolen your lands or contaminated them. How sad this is. How worthwhile it would be for each of us to examine our conscience and learn to say, 'Forgive me!'"

The effort to understand the Maya in the way they portrayed their lives, practices and observations has revealed a great deal about various Maya groups. Epigraphers have brought to life the ancient hieroglyphic texts to the delight of many who appreciate the decoding, offering a glimpse into their views and observations. Experts and enthusiasts turn with wonder to develop the all-encompassing picture of an indigenous people with deep wisdom. The Maya cultivated larger than life ambitions deep in rainforests that to the Old World might have appeared unthinkable and dismissed as inhospitable. Experts turn to the relics left behind, historical testimonies written in Mayan using a Spanish alphabet taught to them by Catholic missionaries, and four of the surviving Maya codices.

Although the Maya wrote a detailed, historical record covering their entire history, the Spanish missionaries hoped to erase this indigenous history. Viewing their documents as heathen, they destroyed the majority of Mayan historical records. The Maya script is considered the most highly developed writing system in the whole of pre-Columbian America and doubtless existed on perishable media. The four remaining examples are the Dresden Codex, the Madrid Codex, the Paris Codex, and Grolier Codex. These codices reviewed the dispatches of Spanish artillery captains from the 1780s and Catholic missionaries who emerged in the territories in the 1700s. They look to the buildings and monuments.

Using different techniques, researchers have studied various aspects of ancient Maya life so that we may find answers. Artifacts made of fired clay that look like figurines, adornments, pottery vessels and ceramics tell a story of Maya that used different sources of clay, which has led to discoveries of different production centers. A review of the stratigraphy to define temporal and spatial frameworks led to a better sense of the chronology of archaeological cultural developments, determining their relationship to what the Maya were developing and experiencing at specific times.

Processual archaeology techniques have been used to build historical frameworks to determine how the Maya people did things, focusing on their cultural ecology and cultural materialism. Settlement pattern studies have informed historical turning points. Post-processual archaeologists have focused on the abilities of individuals, families, and small groups to act and effect change within their larger societies. Their focus on gender, ethnic issues and differences within Maya society have lent much to the evolving picture of the civilization as a whole. University archaeological research with the assistance of government agencies, pioneers, Maya authorities, and project leaders from the likes of the Tikal Project and Cozumel Project have advanced our understanding of historical facts.

Accurately piecing together the clues the Maya left us requires that archaeologists, epigraphers, anthropologists, and contemporary Mayans who wish to retain a knowledge of their ancestors avoid applying preconceived notions or only the observations of Spanish explorers to what has been unearthed. In fact, by the mid-1970s critical advances proved that the basic premises that archaeologists had posed about the ancient Maya were incorrect. Until then, experts and those who followed the explorations in wonder believed that the Maya were peacefully separated into independent states, mostly conducting trade and sharing knowledge with each other about common concerns, governance, and traditions.

Dr. Arthur Demarest, Ingram Professor of Anthropology at Vanderbilt University and a researcher with decades of experience leading field excavations in the highlands, coasts, and rainforests of Central America, touched on the matter in "Ancient Maya: The Rise and Fall of a Rainforest Civilization." In studying a politically and economically complex ancient society, "the problem has not been a shortage of theories, but rather the scattered, incomplete, and contradictory nature of the archaeological evidence." New discoveries continue to topple traditional views and question held interpretations. Due to more thorough analysis and new findings, a new, more realistic picture of the Maya has since emerged.

The Maya were much more complex than previously held theories supposed. Based on the discovery of hieroglyphics that preserved a different picture of the lives of the Maya people, experts have determined that the Maya city-states were regularly in a state of clashes with one another. The reasons are varied; carved stones tell the story as written by Maya rulers the way they wished to be remembered. Excavations in eastern Mexico, Belize, Guatemala, western Honduras, and El Salvador have vastly improved our understanding of what struggles they faced and how their pursuit of glory, power and transformative shifts shaped them during various eras and in different regions. According to Robert Sharer, Shoemaker Professor of Anthropology at the University of Pennsylvania and Curator of the American Section at the university's Museum of Archaeology and Anthropology, in "The Ancient Maya," historical texts often included additional titles acquired by rulers. These titles expressed their achievements; important events during the dynasties of kings were commemorated in carved texts and scenes, and they were transformed into sacred semi-divine beings upon accession as they took new names identified with deities in recorded texts.

Of course, as one can imagine, an effort has been underway to not only understand the ancient Mayan civilization through texts about Maya rulers but also to paint a more complete picture of the life of the commoners. New findings have sprung up, and we will explore this further in the pages ahead. Elite rulers often carved stone monuments to proclaim prestige and power, emulating the Maya rulers.

The Maya did not emerge from the lost tribes of Israel or Atlantis. Instead, based on overwhelming evidence from linguistics, physical anthropology, and archaeology, ancestors of all New World people, including the Maya, migrated from Asia as nomadic hunters and gatherers. The debate surrounds the timing of their arrival in the Yucatan region and whether the migration across the Bering Strait occurred at about 12,000 BCE, 40,000 BCE or even earlier. Scholars continue to debate whether the Maya made the transition from hunting and gathering to farming villages in the lowland areas they occupied or if it spread into the lowlands from elsewhere. The best evidence for settled agricultural villages growing maize and various vegetables is found in eastern Mesoamerica from the Pacific and Gulf coasts of Mexico, Guatemala, and El Salvador. It shows a combination of cultural practices that included fishing, extensive opportunistic hunting of birds and an increasing reliance on agriculture. From 2000 to 1300 BCE, along the coasts and in some inland zones, evidence shows that there was rapid development of complex societies, while the record in the rainforest lowlands of the Maya area shows little activity.

At the time, the most advanced of the emerging societies was the Olmec civilization. We will discuss the Olmecs briefly in the next chapter since it appears that they had an influence on the Maya people in terms of art, iconography and writing during the Late Preclassic and Classic periods. While the debate still lingers, many consider the Olmec influence so widespread that Olmec is considered the mother culture of the Americas. For instance, while the Maya are credited for the widely used concept of zero, the Olmecs are credited for having conceptualized it originally.

Today's Pan-Maya movement recognizes and honors the voices of Mayan ancestors. As a result of their history, Mayan identity now transcends birthplace or languages, and youth with Mayan heritage are learning how to write their names in the now deciphered hieroglyphs of their predecessors. In many of the countries where Maya live, they are contributing members of their societies and are helping to reconstruct their ancient cities and their pasts. Maya shaman-priests make pilgrimages to Momostenango in Guatemala to learn their ancient sacred calendar maintained there for the past 500 years. Their contemporaries struggle against marginalization, and they continue their efforts to revitalize the language, spirituality and native knowledge that has emerged from all the studies that their ancestors have provoked. While the Maya have dealt with severe circumstances and marginalization under authoritarian conditions in many of the countries where they make their communities, they continue to show the resilience of an indigenous culture that helps them maintain their identity separate from global identities.

However, it is also interesting to note that according to assistant professor of anthropology at Brown University Andrew K. Scherer, in "Mortuary Landscapes of the Classic Maya: Rituals of Body and Soul," contemporary Maya do not share a universal perspective as to whether they are or are not the descendants of the people that archaeologists define as the Classic Maya. He found that while some of the archaeological sites, such as the Great Plaza of Tikal, are places of pilgrimage for contemporary ritual performances, none of the various Q'eqchi, Kaqchikel, Chol, and Tzeltal men he worked with on his archaeological projects over the years saw themselves particularly connected to the past. "They expressed fascination…yet still perceived these people as distant, remote, and, in many respects, a supernatural other."

Chapter Three
Different Periods of Maya History

Many authorities on the subject generally agree that the early history of the Mayan civilization is obscure. There just isn't enough evidence. However, from the evidence that they have analyzed and interpreted, scholars and field experts have created 3 major epochs to denote chronological intervals. The Pre-Classic Era is considered to represent the Maya developments from 2000 BCE-250 BCE. The Classic Era includes 250 CE-900 CE. The Post-Classic Era includes 900 CE to 1697 CE. The descriptions will be used throughout the book.

The Maya were part of a Mesoamerican history influenced by Olmecs from the Gulf coastal plain, the Zapotec and Mixtec of Oaxaca in the West, and the cultures in Teotihuacan and Tula in the northwest, including the Aztecs and Huaxteca. It is widely considered that the exchange between the Olmecs and cultures of the Pacific corridor led to the rise of the Mayan civilization in both Central America and Mexico.

According to Professor of Political Science at California Polytechnic State University at San Luis Obispo, Craig Arceneaux writes in "Democratic Latin America," Olmec archaeological sites all point to the existence of a significant ancient trade network. The Mayan civilization was intimately tied to the Olmecs, a civilization which essentially vanished in 300 BCE. The Maya acted as middlemen in trade networks developed by the Olmecs. The Olmecs built the first American pyramid in La Venta, located in the present-day Mexican state of Tabasco.

Additionally, the Olmecs grew their wealth from exporting maize, chocolate, exotic skins, and hides. They imported obsidian and other exotic materials like serpentine and jade. Olmec jade in Maya monumental architecture traces the influence of the Olmec. The name *Olmec* refers to "dweller in the land of rubber", for the rubber trees that flourished in their area. They made the first bouncing balls from the tropical Castilla elastica tree.

A pre-Columbian ball game figured prominently in the Maya creation myth, depicting ball-playing good "Hero Twins" who outwit and defeat the evil gods of the underworld to prepare for the dawning of the world and rebirth of the maize god. These twin heroes were reborn as the sun and moon, signaling the dawning of a new age. Evidence shows that the legend of the twin heroes was reenacted at least once during a ritual sacrifice at the Maya site of Tikal, where a boy and man were sacrificed in order to shed their human individuality and assume the power associated with the myth to claim entry into the sacred world. By imitating the actions of gods, some experts believe that the Maya considered they could live again in the time of origin.

Among many other customs and practices, the Maya also followed in the tradition of Olmecs in exchanging symbols of prestige with neighbors to the south on the isthmus. In return, they received knowledge of the arts of metallurgy and ceramics.

Warfare played a critical role in defining Maya policies, organization and the extent of their power beginning in the Pre-Classical Era. Some experts claim that some warfare events were actually reenactments of the hero twins and other ancient myths in order for Maya rulers to humble their enemies and dismantle the political power of their rival rulers. The creation myth legitimized their actions by perpetuating these myths and the struggle for power.

Warfare influenced a great deal of their decisions in the Classic Period. It reinforced the stratification of society, centralized political authority, and expanded resources, labor, and prestige. Taking captors was a regular feature of Class-period texts extolling the achievements of kings.

Scientists believe that the Maya were hardly a humanitarian culture since they put war at the center. This included behavior such as the capture, torture, and slaughter of enemy soldiers, leaders, and kings. Mayan art and writing featured scenes of captured enemies cut open while alive and pleading with their captors. Through the work undertaken by Thomas Sowell in "Conquests and Cultures: An International History," Maya warriors wore coats decorated with the shrunken heads of their victims. Additionally, Jack David Eller, Associate Professor of Anthropology at the Community College of Denver, concluded in "Introducing Anthropology of Religion: Culture to the Ultimate," that many of the sacrificial practices performed by both the Aztec and Maya, some of which are truly grim, were done for political and spiritual gains. Sacrifice maintained the power of supernatural beings and the social roles of the king and priests to preserve an economy of life, where vitality was spent here to invest it in the supernatural order they so firmly believed in.

This power gave the king and priest authority over other men. Engaging in war was a form of ritual for the Maya. Based on research published by M. Kathryn Brown and Travis W. Stanton in "Ancient Mesoamerican Warfare," it may have been ritually based and timed to coincide with celestial events. Evidence suggests that raiding for the purpose of capturing sacrificial victims was quite common. In other words, economic and political competition depended on warfare that reenacted the gods in Maya ideology battling against and conquering other gods but applied to different dynasties in city-states. Rulers were considered reincarnated gods, and victory was a huge component to their perceived strength and might.

Since war and rituals were the tools of kings, according to Dr. Brian Fagan and Nadia Durrani in "People of the Earth: An Introduction to World Prehistory," the kings believed they had a divine covenant with the gods and their ancestors. The ruler was often depicted as the World Tree, which was a conduit by which humans communicated with the Otherworld.

The Maya lived in three separate sub-areas with distinct environmental and cultural differences: the northern Maya lowlands on the Yucatan Peninsula; the southern lowlands in the Peten district of northern Guatemala and adjacent portions of Mexico, Belize and western Honduras; and the southern Maya highlands, in the mountainous region of southern Guatemala. The southern region reached its peak during the Classic Era.

During the Pre-Classic times, Maya chiefdoms emerged along the Pacific coast and southern highlands. Chiefs held special supernatural contracts or abilities, which they relied upon to invoke good or inflict harm. Trade routes linked these chiefdoms and ran from modern-day Mexico to Central America. They were ruled by small groups of powerful elites. Some of their first large city-states (of the sixty or so known city-states throughout the Maya territory) like El Mirador in northern Guatemala date back to the Pre-Classic era. The Danta complex in El Mirador is the largest Mesoamerican pyramid. Excavations at Kaminaljuyu, modern-day Guatemala City and the largest and most powerful Highland Maya site known, revealed the growth of the late pre-Classic Mayan civilization.

In the dry tropical forests of the Yucatan Peninsula, sites were also emerging during the Pre-Classic including Komchen and Yaxuna. People established villages in areas such as Altar de Sacrificios in southwestern Peten, Guatemala, Ceibal in southern Peten, Cuello in northern Belize, Blackman Eddy in Belize, and K'axob in Belize. Nakbe, Uaxactun, and Tikal were growing in the tropical wet lowlands. There is some evidence that people in the highlands and coastal plain areas interacted with lowland people as early as the Pre-Classic Era. One of the first freeway systems in the world ran from El Mirador to Nakbe.

Another Pre-Classic city-state, Nixtun-Ch'ich, thrived in Peten, and boasts the Great Ballcourt architectural complex, thought to have been a key setting for public rituals of integration, competition, and feasting. The court is similar in size to that at Chichen Itza. Interestingly enough, it is the first Maya city built according to a grid pattern. A team of scientists excavating Nixtun-Ch'ich in 1995 determined that, compared to other Maya ancient cities, most were more relaxed in design. According to Timothy Pugh from New York's Queens College, it suggests that some powerful ruler oversaw the design.

The Classic Period is extensively researched. Therefore a few key events from that period are worth mentioning as insights into your exploration of the Mayan civilization. Much of the Classic period has been considered by researchers as a rivalry between the city-states of Tikal and Kalak'mul (modern day Kampache). According to the authors of "The Code of Kings: The Language of Seven Sacred Maya Temples and Tombs," during this period, the number of kingdoms grew rapidly to as many as sixty at the height of lowland Mayan civilization in the eighth century. These kingdoms, beginning in the fifth century, organized themselves into great alliances headed by the kingdoms of Tikal and Kalak'mul. During this time, the alliance between Teotihuacan and Tikal grew.

Tikal at the time was known as Mutul. Its temples rose 230 feet into the sky. Its rulers were from a dynasty of over thirty kings. Evidence shows that they lived in a hierarchical society of nobles, priests, merchants, artisans, warriors, farmers, servants and godlike kings. Their scribes used their mastery of math to record the movements of the sun, moon and plants to chronicle events. Priests conducted rituals to appease the gods to bring success in war and in trade. Fifty thousand to one hundred thousand people lived in Tikal during its prime years. It contained more than 3,000 structures within six square miles.

Stela 29, dating to 292 CE, celebrated the Tikal ruler nicknamed Foliated-Jaguar. Although the pre-Columbia Maya religion knew various jaguar gods and to the Olmec the jaguar was an important part of shamanism, they also sacrificed jaguars. Kitty Emery, an archaeologist at the Florida Museum of Natural History, studied 80,000 animal bones found in 25 Maya trash mounds to map the effects of the Maya rituals of hunting animals over 4,000 years. She found that large-animal remains were most plentiful from around 600-900 CE when the Maya population had the highest proportion of elites within its large population. She speculated that the elite demanded more and more in an attempt to prove their status regardless of the worsening environmental conditions.

To the Maya, the jaguar was a symbol of war. In the Popol Vuh, Maya gods with jaguar attributes are underworld gods. According to Nicholas J. Saunders in "Icons of Power: Feline Symbolism in the Americas," the Jaguar God of the Underworld was not only the most common image on Classic Maya shields, but it was the most common main head on temple structures. He further explained that Classic Maya rulers took jaguar names in various city-states and that Mayan gods and kings wore jaguar-skin kilts, capes, and sandals. According to Rod

Preece in "Animals and Nature: Cultural Myths, Cultural Realities," Maya exported jaguar pelts for luxury uses.

For an interesting analysis of how the Maya moved away from worshiping animals and conveying that through idolizing them in royal names and in other ritualistic practices, the work undertaken by Rod Preece adds some relevant and much-appreciated thought to the topic. Specifically, he made an interesting connection between the Maya as they acquired more capacity for scientific and technological abstraction, while their manner of thought, identity with nature and culture changed. As a result, they acquired the power to master the animals and no longer need to hold them in the same awe, without praying to the animals. Growing rationalism and advancing technology induced their tribal societies to stop their fear of jaguars and all other animals. Their myths and belief systems altered dramatically as their society changed, be they hunter-gatherer, pastoral or feudal, and what type of economy they established.

Classic Mayan civilization city-states like Uaxactún, Copán, Bonampak, Dos Pilas, Calakmul, Palenque and Río Bec each held between 5,000 and 50,000 people. During this period, the Mayan culture built stone temples, pyramids, and central markets. Their kings grew to become semi-divine, nobles ran fiefdoms, and the wealthy upper class grew. Status was marked by jewelry and adornments, and the nobility drank chocolate. Peasants worked the fields and lived in the forests. They instituted transformative improvements to agricultural techniques and expanded their long distance trade. Since slash and burn was not sustainable, they moved to raised-field and hydraulic systems to increase the amount of land under cultivation and yields.

Evidence that divine kingdoms within polities lorded over smaller sites has helped understand some of the provincial relationships and also some of the inscriptions that have been found. While scholars have spent a great deal of effort to understand the nature of the relationships between all 60 of the city-states, a few key phrases in inscriptions have provided some more clues. According to Valerie Hansen and Ken Curtis in "Voyages in World History, Volume I," some rulers are said to be someone else's king, indicating there was an overlord. Since one of the central goals of Maya city-states was to lord over each other's dominions and to increase their territory, the Maya devoted a great deal of resources to war. In field studies, one Classic period site named El Cayo was lorded over by the larger divine kingdom of Piedra Negras.

In October 1929, on their first day's flight, American aviator Charles Lindbergh piloted the Chairman of the Division of Historical Research of the Carnegie Institution of Washington Alfred V. Kidder and archaeologist Oliver Ricketson, Jr. over the little known or unexplored areas of ancient Maya territory into El Cayo followed by the ruins of Tikal, discussed earlier. They ended up in Chichen Itza the following day. What made Lindbergh's flight to the region so fascinating was that Kidder was a pioneer in the use of aerial survey and photography in archaeology. Charles Lindbergh had successfully completed his famous trip across the Atlantic two years earlier. According to the digitized archive of the full text of an administrative report dating from July 1, 1929, to June 30, 1930, published by the Carnegie Institute, they found the five-day flight results most satisfactory: several unrecorded ruins were observed, and they were able to ascertain the benefits of future intensive air surveys and for landing in the interior during future investigations deep in the Maya jungles.

Articles like "Lindy to Seek Lost, Ancient Cities From Air," which was published in the Chicago Tribune, appeared in newspapers and magazines before and after the rare early flight over the Yucatan. "Popular Science" in January 1930 explored the topic of the Maya, including the key findings that Ricketson had discovered in Chichen Itza only a few years before flying over the very round tower ruins that the Maya had supposedly used as an astronomical observatory.

Eventually, the center of the Mayan civilization shifted to the city-states of the Yucatan Peninsula and Chiapas. Chichen Itza dominated the Mayan civilization during the end of the Classic era and Post-Classic period. In the eighth century, it is estimated there were 14 million Maya, mostly south of Yucatan. Settlement patterns show that many abandoned the southern city-states; moving north, they continued their religious and social order. During the unsettled Postclassic conditions caused by tribal warfare and population movements, many groups of invaders vied for political power in central Mexico until the Toltecs achieved dominance in the tenth century CE followed by the great Aztec Empire.

Often considered the real Indiana Jones, Maya expert Dr. Arthur Demarest, through years of extensive well-thought research, has built a great understanding of the shifts in Maya history. During the Classic period, they practiced K'uhul Ajaw, which translates to "Holy Lords," to promote a system of competitive states substantiated by religious, military and political power that was heavily dependent on political ideology and the power of religion and ritual. Huge ceremonies occurred in great plazas and patronage networks were developed to supply sacred goods and feast provisions. During the Post-Classic period, power was more distributed and divided; status-enhancing ideology was relatively reduced. The economies shifted to a more long-distance exchange of commodities.

In terms of the collapse that occurred during the Post-Classic period that has been the preoccupation of many in the field, Demarest considers that it is first important to specify that the Maya culture did not collapse. In fact, it continued in the Post-Classic era and beyond in the northern lowlands. It was the system that they built that collapsed. That led to population shifts and the abandonment of city-states, especially in the southern lowland. The traditions continued, despite the centralized political and economic declines. He found that the general traits of Classic Maya political and economic systems greatly invested in massive rituals, discontinuous and unstable systems of alliance between polities, warfare that was usually for the purpose of dynastic control and elite status rivalry, and other notable traits. As a result, not only did the increased integration of the Mayan civilization with shared alliances, internal hierarchies, and wide-ranging trade become a strength, it also became a weakness.

Religion and ritual used to sustain power as a source of strength caused tension as the growth of the elite class increased demands for products and services. Overuse, despite the fact that the Maya adjusted to sensitivities and subsistence environmental challenges, led to crisis. Factors that led to the crisis include increased war, status rivalry, destroyed rivers and overused infrastructures and a larger, more contentious elite class pressuring for growth from the non-elite.

In 2005, the most important thing Demarest had ever discovered led him to the shocking truth that the normal ways of Maya warfare had changed near the end of the Classic period. The conquerors who invaded the ancient Maya city of Cancuen had destroyed the city. Around 800 CE they had methodically destroyed the palace and its monuments and rounded up the rulers, members of the court, and killed a group of men, women, and children en masse. Researchers had found as many as 50 skeletons in a sacred pool and other places; these individuals had been murdered and dismembered. Cancuen was known to have been one of the abandoned cities during the period; the other neighboring river cities had also been abandoned within ten years of Cancuen's fall. Other experts agree that this was a sharp departure in Mayan warfare and became characteristic of the Mayan civilization in the collapse period.

In his essay "War, Peace and the Collapse of a Native American Civilization: Lessons for Contemporary Systems of Conflict," Demarest explained that the Classic Mayan civilization gradually shifted over a millennium from a system of controlled conflict to one of conquest states and finally to unrestricted and highly destructive warfare. Using Dos Pilas in 761 CE as an example of warfare that had evolved from dynastic conquest to militaristic anarchy, he concluded that the equilibrium that had been maintained with stable relations had been disrupted. The stability previously held was astonishing given their ecological adaptation, economics, and the restrictions the Maya maintained on combat and collateral damage. Dos Pilas showed the growth of a self-interested elite that, for the purpose of pursuing political gains, used more aggressive tactics, increased the frequency of conflicts, and showed a growing disregard for the canons of war that the Maya had traditionally honored.

Thinking along those lines, it's conceivable that the decisions the Mayan civilization made throughout its spread out city-states to choose building more temples, conducting more sacrifices and ignoring the real problems that started to plague them didn't exactly fill the Maya non-elite (and those within the elite circles who depended on the pre-crisis system) with confidence. The status quo wasn't working. As you read other accounts about the decline of the Maya, also consider some of the new findings included in Chapter Five that will inform your own thoughts on the

Mayan civilization that you may have considered in your discovery process.

Chapter Four
Larger Than Life

Plenty of people who have put some thought to the life and times of the Maya people walk away wondering about how they could accomplish so much in their environments. The Maya seemed to be able to maintain a seamless relationship between ecological resources and nature, a highly religious society governed by a divine king, and a system of power struggles. Yet, in many ways, their larger than life existence makes it no wonder that understanding of the way they lived their lives sent themselves into a death spiral. Would anyone truly continue to trust rulers and their reinforcing elite if in the face of the crises they faced? The answer, culturally, was: (1) to continue with rituals; (2) request more supply and service demanding ceremonies, and (3) to expect more moral and required support to kings geared toward having to establish might and victory in perpetual need of expansion.

The list of crises that the Maya began to face during their decline, all of which have been debated for some time, include: drought, environmental overuse and disasters, overpopulation, disruption of trade routes, excessive growth driven by elite, a restlessness that brought a general conflict to the area, peasant revolts, overpopulation, and epidemics.

To know the Maya culture is not just to rely on portrayals that elevate the Maya shaman and the Maya respect for nature above other civilizations. Sure, other civilizations have dealt with their own priorities, conflicts, and internal and external threats to their way of life, and governance policies that don't adequately address societal concerns. Is it true, like some have interpreted, that we can turn to the Maya to relearn from ancestral knowledge how to avoid disconnecting from the world around us, even though we cannot simplify their story conveniently and only notice the seemingly positive attributes of their civilization?

Although that is a question that can fill an entire book, what we can handle here is the possibility that many civilizations have had a powerful, increasingly driven elite that led to a disconnect with previously held traditions for the sake of the status-minded. Then, we may at least be honest that the Maya themselves moved away from the very knowledge that is often portrayed as uniquely Maya in origin: a connection with the sacred in everything. With further exploration, without taking away from the Maya potential for treating their ecological world with a sacredness that brought an awareness of a oneness with nature and the cosmos, that lack of separateness from nature, seeds, and a stewarded environment may have less to do with integral Maya-ness. It may have to do with indigenous designs based on living close to the land and can be seen as a shared value by many indigenous groups around the world before power and expansion ambitions drive the very system into chaos. It's a thought.

Now, their very larger than life civilization is the subject of much awe and criticism. Here we'll explore only some of it, including their architecture and manipulation of their environment, their use of cosmology and religion for the purposes of war and peace, their kings, their myths, and how their practices were shaped by their beliefs and worship.

Maya planned cities to conform to their natural settings rather than more typical grid-like cities, generally speaking. This distinguished them. Additionally, they had a complex understanding of astronomy that touched many aspects of their lives. They built elaborate cities and relied on diviners, shamans, priests, and kings granted divine powers for their economy, safety and preservation. However, by the end of their civilization, they faced soil depletion. In early parts of their civilization, they had moved away from slash and burn methods to developing terracing, drainage and irrigation systems that improved the fertility of their soil and retention of much-needed water.

According to Maya expert Dr. Arthur Demarest, one of the reasons why the Maya were able to conform to their environments was that most of the sub-regions of the lowlands limited the role of rulers and kingdoms. In general, most decisions about agriculture and land use were made at the level of communities, where those who had the most field experience were. Within these communities, they had the most knowledge about the sensitive and fragile variations of the forest soils, slopes and karst landscape, including draining conditions.

Given that scholars and scientists have found that their kings acted like gods, it would seem that if they were more preoccupied with the power they wielded over the people rather than desperation and matters of public concern, it was a good thing. If their ordained status and the fervent war spirit to appear godlike took precedence, then Maya populations had good cause to repopulate in other areas if internal rivalries and societal damage was on the rise. According to William Fash, the Bowditch Professor of Central American and Mexican Archaeology and Ethnology in Harvard University's Department of Anthropology, the Maya kings had attributes of the supernatural. They considered human blood, the most sacred thing they could offer the gods to repay them for the blood debt of their own creation.

Since bloodletting, human and animal sacrifices played an important part of the king's strategic thinking, when the gods didn't respond to their ritual and ceremonial problem solving, they might have lost power in the eyes of those being ruled. Studies reveal higher than expected soil erosion linked to farming practices and rapid land use by pioneers. While many of the Maya structures are still visible today, much to the delight of Maya enthusiasts who travel to the temples, research shows that the civilization's impact on the climate is also still visible today. Researchers from the University of Texas synthesized old and new data to find that the Maya's advanced urban and rural infrastructures altered ecosystems of global importance indicated by erosion, human land-use changes and periods of instability. The scientists consider the changes both good and bad. "Historically, it's common for people to talk about the bad that happened with past environmental changes, such as erosion and climate change from deforestation," lead author Tim Beach, the C.B. Smith Sr. Centennial Professor of Geography and the Environment said. "But we can learn a lot from how Maya altered their environment to create vast field systems to grow more crops and respond to rising sea levels."

To share his ideas of grandeur, the Maya King K'inich Janaab Pacal—Pacal the Great (615-683 BCE)—revitalized architectural structures in Palenque, two hundred and fifty miles to the west of Tikal, at a time when they developed temporary alliances with Maya individual city-states like Tikal, Copan, Kalak'mul, and Caracol during the Classic period. According to Dr. Brian Fagan and Nadia Durrant in "People of the Earth: An Introduction to World Prehistory," Tikal had few allies in the immediate vicinity, maintained friendly relations with Palenque and Copan, but had a deep rivalry with Calakmul. The extreme rivalry culminated in warfare and constant shifts in allegiance between Tikal, Calakmul, and Caracol.

Pacal inherited the throne from his mother Lady-Zac-Kuk, who served for a time as a ruler as a result of Pacal's young age of 12 at the time that he would have claimed the throne. She claimed the throne for her son when Palenque did not have a known heir. He deified himself and declared his mother as the living embodiment of the first mother who created humans and gods, legitimizing his rule over Palenque as the son of a goddess. Three pyramid complexes were designed by his son Chan Bahlum (Snake-Jaguar) after he took the throne. Experts see Pacal as the founder of the Palenque dynasty, but his son as a consolidator who made sure the dynasty continued. His pyramids towered over his father's. The pyramids in Palenque have revealed a great deal about the mystery of this dynasty that are riveting and worth further reading. For one thing, they used cinnabar to coat the images found within their temples to prevent looting, since it is poisonous to the touch.

While some pyramids were considered shaman training centers, the way that pyramids were built in many of the Maya city-states, including the ones mentioned earlier, Chichen Itza and Uaxactun, reveals the stellar planning that the Maya brought to their endeavors. Uaxactun is one of the earliest astronomical alignments to be recognized in Maya architecture. Overall, the Maya magnified their pyramids by positioning them based on astronomical observations. At sunset during the spring and fall equinoxes, Chichen Itza's pyramid casts a shadow on itself that aligns with a carving of the head of the Maya serpent god. The pyramid is situated according to the sun's location during these equinoxes, and as the sun sets, the serpent appears to slither down into the earth.

The Maya strongly believed in the influence of the cosmos on daily life. Their Dresden Codex appears to be mostly astronomical as an almanac stuffed with information about different celestial bodies. While much study has shown that Venus was the main focus of their attention, according to Heather Couper and Niegel Henbest in "The Story of Astronomy: How the Universe Revealed its Secrets," astronomical historian Ed Krupp thinks we could be in danger of being misled. He argues that the sun and the moon were also very important to their culture and Venus was probably no less and no more important than other key celestial objects. Archaeoastronomer Clive Ruggles suggests that "In the Maya case, the fact that we happen to have these codices, like the Dresden Codex, shows what incredible detail they went into correlating the different cycles of eclipses and so on. There's actually nothing in the architecture that would really convince us of that." However, according to Couper and Henbest, Chichen Itza is one blatant exception at the time of equinoxes.

Think huge! It's no wonder that many of their city centers were interpretations of sacred mountains that acted as royal tombs and that their temples symbolized cave entrances to the underworld or that they reenacted the creation of the Maya universe in ball courts that they built in their plazas. Most Maya cities had at least one ball court integrated into the ceremonial center of the city.

The maize god died and was reborn in the ball court, and the ball court was described as a crack in the top of a mountain or the carapace of the Cosmic Turtle. People went there to contact their ancestors and consult oracular deities. The Maya and other Mesoamericans sealed alliances there; captured kings were sacrificed there. The Maya are considered the people of the maize. The young maize god was the Maya symbol of world creation and renewal. Themes of sacrifice and resurrection were integral to the pre-Columbian world view. Corn was a way of life. In the Popol Vuh, the maize god was central to the birth of the sun and creation of the world. The Maya performed many rituals surrounding maize.

As mentioned earlier, war also played a central role. Their architecture reflected their penchant for warfare and showed in the defensive walls in many of their cities. During the Classic period, the Maya built their cities on hilltops and the archaeological record shows that war became more intense and frequent towards the time of the Classic collapse as they warred for dominance. Kings fought to take one another captive to be tortured and sometimes beheaded, as were other captives, in a ritual reenactment of the decapitation of the Maya maize god by the pantheon's death gods.

Maya read the skies to predict the fate of empires. Priests advised rulers. Their origin of the world cosmologies are considered elaborate and add to the enigma of the people. Their heavens were composed of layers each with their own gods. Their earlier animism, which outdates many organized religions in communing with the spirits and animals of nature, is reflected in many of their interpretations of the sky, earth, themselves, their rulers, and their place and dominance in the social order. The Popol Vuh described a natural world where there is no separation of the sacred from the mundane, and everything had a sacred element. They conducted many rituals and dances by channeling the dynamic forces of the supernatural into the human sphere. In keeping with their cyclical nature of time and belief in predestination, they conducted wars during important anniversaries of past events or auspicious positions of the planets. They interpreted life as highly-ordered cycles of creation, aggression, and fragmentation.

Applying their world view to their hierarchical societies, their kings were not equal, as the size and power of the individual polities change and more powerful kings took on special titles to indicate their elevated status. For example, kings of Tikal used the title *kaloomte'* to denote an especially powerful king. The loss of a king during a coup was a big blow since the *k'uhul ajaw* to the ancient Maya was the living link between this world and the supernatural, necessary for the continuation of the institutions they held such strong blind faith in. The polity was usually preserved, however, despite capture, and another ruler would ascend the throne. Kings were glorified for their military victories and conquests brought more prestige.

Interestingly enough, when we consider the development of two calendars (the Calendar Round 260-day sacred year and their 365-day secular year), even the numbers were sacred. Each day had 4 identifiers that referred to both calendars with a number and a name. Their Long Count calendar started with the base date August 11 or 13, 3114 BCE, in which they grouped numbers reading left to right then downward into *bak'tuns, k'atuns, tuns, winals* and *k'ins*, with the latter was one day as the basic unit of time. They combined into groups of 20 which made one *winal*. A *tun* was 360 days. Twenty *tuns* made a *k'atun* or 7,200 days. Patron deities represented *k'atuns* and expressed a prophecy of the future. Twenty *k'atuns* equaled 1 *bak'tun* or 144,000 days. One grand cycle for the Long Count was 13 *bak'tun* or 5,139 solar years, and it marked another cycle in the passing of history from the beginning of time. The last one ended on December 10, 2012.

These measured cycles were cosmic patterns that pervaded all aspects of existence and allowed the Maya to engage with the supernatural. According to Lynn Foster in the "Handbook to Life in the Ancient Maya World," the intervals timing the movements of celestial bodies, therefore, paralleled the activities of humans within Maya societies. Think big!

While they lived large, the history of their kings, battles, deities, origin cosmology and culture is expansive and worth studying further. A culture that believed in 160 deities, conducted blood sacrifices of animals and humans, believed in the spirits of the forests and evil winds that led to disease, conducted elaborate rituals for the dead and other pivotal life thresholds, among other enigmatic patterns of living, come from the people who were made from maize by the Hero Twins. Their deeply spiritual lives included healing traditions like shamanism that is still practiced among some modern day descendants. And although their contributions include the first known tear gas, which they unknowingly invented when they were forced to defend themselves during the Spanish Conquest against cannons, horses, and gunpowder, their contributions to humankind's understanding of how conquest of their indigenous group would impact the world from then on helps us reflect on the causes and effects of their subjugation.

Would a Pope have apologized for the treatment of the Maya in any other time of history, as Pope Francis did? History shows us how the Maya lived and developed over the course of their increasingly more sophisticated civilization, handling many of the same conflicts and social ills that we see in the world today. Authorities and enthusiasts look back at history and the events and question what these events did in regards to overall humanity. They help us see the complex web humans weave and how fragile civilizations might be, despite ambitions, beliefs, victories, defeats and tributes and help us reflect on the past and present in a more informed approach. As a civilization, the Maya contributed to our understanding of astronomy, architecture and city planning, math, calendrics, ecology, medicine, writing, technology, politics, anthropology, sociology, commerce, and the arts. They are credited for making the first pressurized hydraulic system. They help us understand their traditional and evolving thinking and ways of life.

Although they were shaped by internal cultural processes and interacted with their contemporary neighbors, evidence shows that before the Spanish Conquests and their first encounters with Europeans, Mesoamerican cultures like the Maya developed independently of the Old World in a barter economy with sophisticated trade networks. They built pyramids and temples that continue to captivate the world and help us look at the world around us in appreciation of what it means to survive, consider our place in the world, and the impact of being part of any particular civilization. The human experience is so vast, and our perpetual thirst to gain an appreciation of our histories and insights is so vast when it comes to inner- and inter-cultural conflicts of interests, that we continue to expand our knowledge on the topic by considering a wide range of perspectives.

Chapter Five
New Findings

Exciting new clues about the ancient Maya continue to surface and help us question, confirm or add to what we already know.

A new stele (a carved stone monument that are a trademark of the late Classic Period) was found by a team of archaeologists at El Achiotal in Guatemala in 2015. It may depict a local vassal lord who was installed by a warrior ruler named Siyaj K'ahk' ("Fire is Born") from Teotihuacan. In 378 CE, his forces arrived in the Maya lowlands to depose the rulers of Tikal to establish a new political order across the Maya territories. The name of the vassal lord (*ajaw*) is still unknown. However, since the translators determined it was erected in celebration of a 40 year anniversary, they counted backward from the date inscribed on the stele, which was November 22, 418 BCE. 378 BCE was the year that Siyaj K'ahk' installed new leadership in Tikal and changed the Maya political system. Epigrapher David Stuart from the University of Texas at Austin said that they had no idea that El Achiotal had been sucked into the new world order. The well-documented battle between the two great Maya superpowers Tikal and Calakmul had been termed by historians as an ancient Cold War.

In 2015, more insight into the eating and prestige habits of various social classes emerged after a researcher from the University of Florida studied 22,000 ancient animal bones stored at the Florida Museum of Natural History. Since most of what we know about the Mayan civilization relates to kings, queens, and elaborate architecture, it's a key revelation as to how the tens of thousands of middle-class and lower-income Maya lived. By tracing the movement of animals and their resources, they found that the distribution of food and access to species varied among cities and social classes. Animals were emblems of status, royalty and symbolic of gods. They found that middle-ranking elites used the widest variety of animals while royalty and high-ranking elites selected jaguars and crocodiles from more select symbolic and prestigious animals. Poor villagers mostly ate fish and shellfish and kept a wide variety of animals. They concluded that the differences in predominant species showed the city-states likely had different trade partners and unique cultural identities.

Another clear window into the lives of Maya commoners appeared to open for archaeologists excavating the ancient village of Ceren in El Salvador that was preserved in pristine conditions because of a volcanic eruption from Loma Caldera. According to their studies published in 2015, the residents of Ceren were not lorded over by their society's rulers. Farmers went about their lives with virtually no strong-arming by elite royalty. Since many Mayan archaeological records show a top-down society where the elite made most political and economic decisions, it is quite extraordinary to see they lived with no control by the elites. They had freedom to make crucial decisions about crops, religion, and family.

2016 reports reveal more evidence of the long tradition of child sacrifices, which was confirmed after radiocarbon dating of 9,566 human bones found from 2008 to 2010 on a cave floor in Belize's Midnight Terror Cave. The study indicated that the bones had been deposited one or a few bodies at a time in the cave over about a 1,500 year period. Since ancient Maya considered inner cave areas with water sources sacred spaces, it suggests the bodies were placed there intentionally as offerings to Chaac, the rain, water and lightning god. This is the second underground cave with the first being Chichen Itza to reveal children and teens were also killed during human sacrifices. No evidence was found that they died of natural causes or had been buried.

The discovery of something called a *rejollada* by a Canadian archaeologist in April 2016 has contributed to our understanding of how ancient Maya farmed in the naturally unfriendly Yucatan. It is a large circular sinkhole with soil at the bottom in the natural limestone bedrock that often contains moist soil. They vary in size; some of the ones they excavated could fit a soccer field. They were a life saver for the ancient Maya in terms of gardening and growing edibles. These **rejolladas** and cenotes (natural water-filled sinkholes) would have made gardening and other agricultural pursuits possible.

Conclusions

As mentioned by many experts who study the Mayan civilization, the demise and decline of their system led to a great escape from the territories that had once thrived. While the traditional elements, rituals, and practices did not remain static after the colonial period, they have continued to change today. Studies that focus on contemporary Maya communities inform these generations to preserve the legacy of the Mayan civilization and help gain an understanding of the past and present. While some books focus on the resistance to the outside forces of the Maya of today, others stress that it has only been recent that the Maya themselves have been able to participate in the educational process of gathering and publishing research about the ancient Mayan civilization.

As those who are interested among the Maya themselves rediscover the achievements and meaning of the pre-Columbian Mayan civilization, it engenders a sense of pride and self-worth and a sense of protection at a time when looting of ancient Maya sites concerns archaeologists and enthusiasts. Although some archaeological teams have experienced the looting, dangerous claims to the artifacts stem from local groups who defy those who are put in charge of safekeeping these excavated relics. An example can be found when internationally-acclaimed archaeologist Peter Matthews and his team were beaten while attempting to preserve a Maya altar, found at the Late Classic site of El Cayo in 1993. The lines are not always clear; the thriving antiquities market threatens to prevent the Maya from reclaiming a better understanding of their past even as they occupy the same territories of their ancestors as citizens of the various countries that hold authority over them.

Modern Maya in Guatemala and Chiapas practice a rich textile art that derives from their ancestors. Their color choices still relate to the past. Reading accounts from Mayans themselves who have been affected by the violence and cultural changes that occurred over time is a necessity. It helps us understand not only the scientific exploration of the Mayan civilization but expose us to the views of individuals who are relating their interpretations of their own past. As Victor Montejo wrote in his book, "Voices from Exile: Violence and Survival in Modern Maya History, "Our stories and knowledge have been treated as data to be processed into ethnographies by and for the academic interpreters." As a Maya anthropologist, he wrote his book in an effort to revitalize Maya culture. He wrote it for an audience that is interested in understanding the modern efforts of those who have tried to replicate their culture in various spaces that were once either Maya territory or altogether outside of the traditional motherland. He focused on the inheritors of that great civilization and conveyed that the Maya people can offer an understanding of a deeper relationship with nature and the universe to Western thinkers with "new ways to understand our current ecological and economic crisis."

The Maya have made major contributions to Central American countries where they live, and their traditions and rituals continue to find expression in modern hybrid-Christian-Maya faith. As history has shown, the value of ancient relics continues to stand the test of time. By continuing explorations, exposing ourselves to new scientific research, and including Maya oral histories, we can gain a better understanding of the Maya experience as it relates to our interest in our further discovery of how vast our human experience truly is. While cultures change and systems decline, our sense of wonder for piecing together a fuller picture of a culture emerges when new focus is brought to the Mayan civilization.

In seeking lost treasures and securing them from those who only intend to minimize our shared past, we dare to consider that although the norms of our culture may be different today, the questions and problems and solutions may not be so different from the ancient Maya. The way we address the fears and powerlessness of being human may make us turn toward the spiritual or seek practical guidance while practicing a new way of life. However, in looking at the Maya who wanted to capture the strength of their gods, to become divine, and turn to something larger than human to take away human problems or to gain more power in handling these problems is something that humans still practice in various ways today. We might learn to respect beliefs all the while understanding how fragile and immense humanity is, especially when worlds collide.

Printed in Poland
by Amazon Fulfillment
Poland Sp. z o.o., Wrocław